ADIRONDACK REIDINGS - VOLUME IV

Revised and Expanded Edition

HELLO . . .

ADIRONDACKER !

By

Edwin A. Reid

Reid Publications
Wanakena, NY 13695
Brant Lake, NY 12815

ADIRONDACK REIDINGS VOLUME IV
HELLO ADIRONDACKER

Original Edition 1987
Revised and Expanded Edition 1998

ISBN 1-890072-04-4

Grateful acknowledgements to Maurya Reid, Robert Snyder, Paula Jay, Sandra Kocher, Jack Leadley and Scott Yeager for their illustrations.

Cover Art: Paula Jay

Published by:
Reid Publications

591 Beaver Pond Road
Brant Lake, NY 12815

P. O. Box 36
Wanakena, NY 13695

Other books by Edwin A. Reid
in the **ADIRONDACK REIDINGS** series:.

MAKE THEM HUNTERS
REACH FOR THE WILDS
PACKBASKET COUNTRY
ADIRONDACK WE CELEBRATE
CAMPS AND CRITTERS
WHERE THE PAVEMENT ENDS (forthcoming)

Printed by Daamen, Inc.
P.O Box 97
West Rutland, Vt.
05777

Hello Adirondacker!

TABLE OF CONTENTS

Dedication
Preface
Adirondacker's Soliloquy 1
Highway Adirondacker.......... 14
Spring Snow.......... 16
Skip's Camp.......... 17
Bog River Falls.......... 20
A People Mountain.......... 22
Tamarack in the Stove.......... 25
Pat Dacy's Deadly Saw.......... 26
Life on the Line.......... 29
Wet Woods.......... 30
Woodcutter's Lament.......... 31
The Last Holdouts.......... 35
Moments of Trust.......... 37
Forest Ranger.......... 38
By What Fire Do You Sit?.......... 39
Orphan Land.......... 42
Bark Not For Me.......... 44
Here No More.......... 45
Bridges Gone.......... 46
Brother Winters.......... 49
Apples of Autumn.......... 51
April Snow.......... 53
Swiveled Throne.......... 54
Brother Be Gone.......... 55
The Deer Hunter.......... 57
Venison Gets the Deer.......... 58
Summer Gone.......... 61
So Much Snow.......... 63
River Wild.......... 64
What Peace is This?.......... 65
Give Us Our Song.......... 67
Goodbye Sweet Bliss.......... 69
The Distant Scene.......... 70
A Sure Meal.......... 72
There Goes Jim.......... 73

Floyd Gilmore.......................... 74
Battle at the Bar...................... 75
Gone................................... 77
Devoted Duty........................... 78
Paths Unpaved.......................... 80
Hermit Father.......................... 81
For the Love of an Apple Tree.......... 82
Adirondacker........................... 87
The River Out Front.................... 89
Backroads Rider........................ 91
Deer Guests............................ 93
Lake George: Another Name?............. 97
Big Trees.............................. 99
Horse-Barn Camp........................ 100
A Chickadee Dead....................... 103
A Mountain Face........................ 105
Another Attitude....................... 107
Trillium Tresspassers.................. 108
No Parker Are You...................... 109
Noah John Rondeau...................... 110
A Soldier's Dream...................... 113
A New Acquaintance..................... 115
A Familiar Refrain..................... 117
An Evening Call........................ 119
Here to Stay........................... 120

DEDICATION

To all Adirondackers---native born, native adopted, part-time residents and otherwise who have determined to live a significant portion of their lives close to the wilds in this region, I have dedicated this book.

A specific dedication is made in memory of the late William Toporcer of Colton, New York. Bill and I enjoyed a warm friendship during the last few years of his long and interesting life.

Because of his advanced years this friendship was limited to correspondence and occasional visits to his log home which he shared with his charming wife, Evie. On these visits we shared a wide variety of stories garnered from many experiences in the Adirondacks. We also engaged in long discussions about the writings of famous naturalists, nature writers and woodsmen. Bill's particular favorite was William J. Long whom he championed and admired throughout his life. In 1981 he dedicated his book "GLEANINGS OF STARDUST" to Long with the inscription, "for unforgettable kindness and understanding."

Bill enjoyed telling how he had gained the unique distinction of having made the first recorded ascent of the Gothics, a triple-crested summit, on snowshoes. On the day of the ascent, he met Russell M. L. Carson, who, at the time, was probably the leading authority on first ascents of the High Peaks. He was also the author of PEAKS AND PEOPLE which details various first climbs and the naming of the mountains. When Bill told Carson what he had just done, the author promptly informed him, that as far as he knew, Toporcer's was the first known ascent of the Gothics on snowshoes. Bill was elated. Carson later verified this in a letter.

This feat by Toporcer was never mentioned in any of Carson's many writings on the High Peaks. If he had Bill had no knowledge of it. However, Bill wrote an account of the climb, as Carson had requested in his letter. The short article appeared in High Spots (1-1933-p6), the official publication of the Adirondack Mountain Club.

Soon after the article was published Bill received a short, but pleasing letter from Bob Marshall, the young advocate for wilderness preservation. In it Marshall stated how much he had enjoyed Bill's straight-forward account.

On my last visit I read aloud several of my poems to Bill from the then recently published PACKBASKET COUNTRY. Though the poems were not written in the classic style he loved and wrote so well, his reaction was a positive one. "You have it, Ed," he said with a smile. It made my day, a moment I won't forget. In retrospect, this was our special goodbye. This final farewell, I share with you, the reader, as a happy HELLO.

PREFACE TO REVISED EDITION

I wrote the first edition of HELLO ADIRONDACKER as a winter challenge. Living alone at my camp-home near Wanakena in the northwestern Adirondacks, I decided to work on something to expand the Adirondack Reidings series.

Since I had no one to assist with the typing I thought putting together a small book of poems would solve this problem. I could do it on the Sharp typewriter my brother had given me. The same one I used at the start of the series in 1987. Word Perfect on the Tandy computer was still too complicated for me to decipher. I lost more than I saved.

Not only was this a challenge but an experiment as well. Who buys books of poetry? Of all forms of literary writing volumes of poetry are the most difficult to sell. Who is to blame, the writers, book promoters or a disinterested public? When last was a book of poetry on the best seller list with sales reaching in the many thousands in the span of a year?

But this book of poetry would be about a specific region and its effect on the people who live there. For example, it would attempt to tell of their varied attitudes, insights and reasons for living in the Adirondacks. At least that was part of it. In short, I wanted to say things I thought important and were perhaps best said in a short form of writing. But where did I get off writing an entire book of poetry.

No one has to tell you you're a poet. A sensitivity to situations and the images and ideas it creates is what makes the poet. But I feel the label is ill-fitting because of the preconceived notions of people who think a poet should be one who recites an endless stream of poems from memory. Some do, but mainly a poet is one captures in writing nebulous thoughts and emotions for others to share.

In other words, before it is written it is somewhere in the heart and spirit. Words are just meaningless symbols if they do not strike strings of emotion and understanding. What is a candle without a flame, a bugle without a sustaining blast of air? That's what makes poetry. A heart hides somewhere in the words a poet writes. When they suddenly speak, there is the poem. That's what makes poetry. That's what kept me going. But that's not all of it.

It is one thing to write what you think is poetry, file it away somewhere and forget about it, quite another to prepare it for publication, publish it and expect people to buy it and read it. Since my late teens I had written what I thought were poems. Had I come at last to where I should put out a book of poems? Time was fleeting fast into the bygone of lost opportunities. If the spirit is there go with it. Get it out now or you'll put it off until it's too late. Don't let that happen. There's no going back.

Images and thoughts constantly drift through our minds. Sometimes they sail through on a gentle breeze affording plenty of time to examine, while, at other times, they swoop through like swallows headed south. Poetry is made up of such images and thoughts. It is up to us to catch them however erratic or swift their flight.

Than there are those that linger too long and clutter the mind. One way to open the mind to new images and thoughts is to moor them to the published page. Make them public so they are no longer solely yours. It is a kind of mental housecleaning, a giving-away. Poetry sweeps the mind clean faster than any other kind of writing.

Winter is a good time to tackle such a project. During periods of severe cold, blowing snow, wet and sloppy conditions the outside world is less inviting to most and, in contrast, the cozy indoors feel good. The mind is probably clearer and more open to such a concentrated challenge then during hot days of summer. At the end of the day you have something both solid and spiritual. Like a piece of wood you can hold your poems in hand; wood in the fireplace creates a flaming spirit while the poem read sets the heart afire. This revision also took place in the winter of 1998, warmed both by burning wood in the stove and poems in the chambers of the soul.

Poetry is a spiritual conversation with self, with the world about and with the people and creatures with whom we share it. Not just friends and relatives, but in a broader sense, with people among whom we mingle wherever we go. In trains, buses, planes, stores, theaters, parks. libraries, churches, restaurants, hospitals, trails, streets and highways we share life with people for an instant, for minutes, for hours, for days---and then we separate, disperse in all directions and mix with others we may never encounter again. This is poetry of humanity---the comings together and partings---continually taking place.

At first I kept putting off this revision of HELLO ADIRONDACKER even though the first edition of 500 copies was sold out. I knew it would demand much work, more perhaps than the original. I felt a need to improve and expand. I was unsure, however, when to make the attack for best results.

Surprise. Once revision started I was eager to turn the sod. Find what it hid and discard what I deemed useless or confusing. Revising became a sudden delight with the stage set, the curtain pulled I began the task of rethinking what I had previously written . What stayed, what was scrapped, what was added, what was reworded. I searched for a new harvest.

I revised without dread of retyping. The computer gladly accepted all my changes. It supplied sharp cutters, a close-toothed comb and a fine file. Even the stoutest limbs were easily dissevered. Trimmings vanished into nowhere. Branches sprouted with vigor. Blossomed again. As resident poems were pruned new offerings were planted. With the press of the shift and print buttons, the printer responded with letter-perfect copy. Revision was never easier.

A poem grows as it shrinks. As it is condensed, meaning and depth, expands and deepens. One is more likely to run out of inspiration and patience before a poem is petrified, as it were, into a state of perfection. I dare not make such a claim for any of the poems in this book though I have striven for it.

What I had set out to do in this book was to give identity to a life lived here. Express attitudes not necessarily my own in all cases, but all of those who live here. I hope in some way this has been accomplished. HELLO ADIRONDACKER addresses not only those who live here year round but part-timers and visitors as well. Whatever your status---happy Adirondacking.

MT. DISCOVERY, NEAR ELIZABETHTOWN

AN ADIRONDACKER'S SOLILOQUY

"Hello, Adirondacker," said Mr. Hill as the rural carrier's vehicle stopped, at this turn in the road, by the loaf-shaped mailbox. "I'm John Hill. I bought this place last year. No more city life for us. Just wanted to meet the person who delivers our mail. Took a little time off from the job and working on the house. I was wondering, does living and getting mail here make us Adirondackers too?

"I heard you bought the old place, Mr. Hill," said the carrier as if news of slight concern. "Glad, at last, someone took the farm to live upon, though a farm no more. Glad you made the house as once it looked. Brings back faces of some who once lived there. Adirondackers true now, in a cemetery, about two miles down the road. An Adirondacker you're not because here is where you get your mail. More to it than envelopes stamped and sealed, local newspapers, magazines and catalogs."

"I guess so," said Mr. Hill. "We just wanted a place far enough from the city to be sure it's backwoods country we've got. We don't mind not having another house near or even in sight. Adirondackers or not, we love living here. We're not seasonal transplants, flighty snowbirds that flee at the slightest cool breeze."

Like a spring pole the craggy-faced carrier shot out of the truck, stood by the open door with one arm resting on it while the other hung at his side. They were long arms in good proportion with the tall, slim figure, arms ideal for the carrier's reach from window to roadside mailbox. In voice, firm and stout, he said: "If here you were not born, not much sense calling yourself an Adirondacker. Not a thing of how much land you own. How much you pay in taxes. Or how you vote. Or even how long you live here. Or whatever some say---but being born here.

"This place where you now live," he continued, afire with his own words, as if to convince himself that all he said or was about to say is true, as far as he knew, "was cleared by my folks. My great, great grandfather settled here, when here no others lived or wanted to.

"Pure and simple, just by accident, he found the place. From the start he knew this was where he'd stay. Pines and maples came down to make room for a house, outbuildings and a farm. Never thought much about what the land was good for or not. Stayed because it felt good. Can't grow much on that. Gave up farming for working in the woods, drove a team on icy skids, some at the tannery sweat and some sawyers at the sawmill too. One ran the general store for a while. Some worked on town road crews. Some got into politics. My grandfather was the postmaster for 30 years. In those days the post office was in the store, sometimes even in the postmaster's house. We go back more generations than I know about in these Adirondacks.

"A fading breed are we, sad to none but those who love us. Others come here to live and stay, then gone, or in play return. Live in a house, a camp so grand for sweet weeks of summer; then locked and left to wind, rain and cold. Rigid walls and snowy roof beg for warmth, for company within. In city apartments and houses they wait for winter to bring spring. A call from the city, find someone to shovel off the roof. They want nothing of our long winters! Places left to face the hardship of the land, alone and helpless. Yet Adirondackers they claim to be, when from the land, all they treasure is its summer beauty.

Mr. Hill looked intently at the carrier to state his case to one who made such an issue of contention out of living here.

> "It's true," he said, "we're here for the beauty of the summer ferns, flowers and sparkling lakes, but we're here for the autumn leaves and the winter snow as well. We're here to fish and hunt. Hike the hills. Canoe and boat the beautiful lakes and rivers. Raise our family. Live

frugally. Cut and burn wood. Preserve ruralness. Work wherever we find it. Hell, summer would not be enough for us to love. We want it all. My wife is as much in love with nature as she is with me and I with her."

"Some say, it's back to nature they want." continued the carrier. "Not sure what they mean. Seems more in reverse, pushing nature back, making room for the city they bring with them. I wonder why they come with a big bag of conditions. When I ask, they say, "It's for the beauty we see." But this soon not enough. More city in the country is what they want. More lights, more noise, more of everything. They say it's to improve our way of life. I thought it the other way around. Country no more, beauty no more. Time to move again. For what they came is gone. They say, "So long. Forward our mail." God knows where they go. Place for sale. Have you noticed all the signs?

"Country can't compete with a landscape of sprawling cities, absorbing a continent like a cancer gone wild. Country shrinking. Cities fusing destinies. There's no stopping it, just some resisting it.

"For country peace, they say, is why they come, a peace, they too often cannot long endure. Living on a country road where few others do. So many changes they propose to make it right for them. "Pave the road to our door."

"No more country road. Get rid of the bumps. Get rid of the curves and hills.
Convert a country road into a highway,
smooth and straight, for travel swift.
Get rid of pines that shadow it,
though two hundred years or more
of beauty in their annual rings.
Get rid of the dark.
Light the road like a city street
though here, day or night, few stroll.
Tell me, if to a big city I go, would
they, do the same for me,
demolish big buildings, plant trees and
grasses because I say, I need some
country in the city?

"Wait a minute," shouted Mr. Hill in a roll of laughter."I didn't mean to stir you into an inquiry as to why I am here. Most people don't share your pride, don't care what they're called for living here or there, born here or not. Or what they bring with them. Some welcome it. The house, the lot, the street, the road, the church, the school and the stores---that's the life along with the job and the family. What's beyond is of little or no concern to most. Don't want a label of place when an hour in air whisks one across the state, a day across a continent. Few want to surrender their old identity. Bring their own for you to accept or ignore."

As if he had heard not a word the carrier continued his soliloquy. "Yes, a dying breed are we. Why, I am not sure. Could be because the young love the land less and what is Adirondack? What is Adirondack they do not know. Beyond they go for work, fortune and future. See neither dream nor promise here. Some gone for good, never look back, never come back. Some do, see a new light from afar. Few come back and stay.

"Costume Adirondackers a-plenty we have, big boots, heavy plaid shirts, guide's hat, worn not to suit a trade, nor out of necessity, more as an accessory of visiting here or maybe just to show some what Adirondackers should wear. Thick beards and broad suspenders too, add a touch of old, I guess, as if no sharp blades or electric razors here; as if from a backwoods camp each just emerged at last to free tough skin of sweat, grime and rancid clothes. Glad again civilization's comforts to embrace and lounge with. More to being an Adirondacker than a rustic look draped over skin too soft to claim long, hard days of muscle and back work to gain a right to live, or, is it a wish in time that there they were?

"Adirondacker, not in the show. Can't blame some if this they do not know: the difference is in those who do. Can't blame some, if no relatives, rest in graves, marked or unmarked in forgotten, lonely places near old homesteads once too demanding to make a gain. My grave waits, where my parents and my mate waits, and many others too whose blood we share.

With the gloomy authority of a self-acclaimed patriarch the carrier looked directly at Mr. Hill and made his proclamation: "No matter what you call yourself, an Adirondacker true you're not, until bones of relatives and friends close, or, your very own are buried somewhere in these hills.
Buried where black crows caw
from big pines nearby, a raucous
requiem for you, and lonely loons
call each spring to tell you
they're back. Only then might
I consider it, might I see reason to change, though no guarantee.

"Do I talk like a damn fool of narrow mind, as if, by some special right? I know, aliens all are we, none with a right above the other in this land and beyond.

"I think you're right," said Mr. Hill ."But may I ask, where did your great, great grandpa come from? Could it have been a skip from Vermont, by boat or over ice, across the long-armed lake called Champlain? Or was it with wife and child he came, up from the valley Mohawk? Or maybe he stepped off a crowded ship that brought him across an angry sea from a starving land? Maybe from the North he came, left his country for another so close? From where he came matters little. Remember, those who came here first, no bones of ones close buried here, no common identity anywhere but in the will to find a place, to live a life, as best they could, with what they found and learned to use, as best they could. This, you must admit, an Adirondacker your great, great grandpa was not when first he came. If called such, none would have known what it meant. The name not yet applied to the land or settlers."

"This is true," said the carrier apologetically, "The first Adirondackers were not born here. For such a sad oversight, we forgive them, though, many say, it's not right. We do it just the same because here they planted us. For that we thank them. Some wish they had gone elsewhere.

"From a common crock, they all drank, a wilderness brew found wherever they went and whatever they did. Like thirsty rats, some drank, others less gluttonously, not sure of the brew, not sure, what was enough. As it simmered, as it brewed, so they drank as they dared. O'er mountains of days and nights, o'er decades of hardship, disappointment and sometimes wild delight, deeper seeped the brew, thickened with blood, fired with heart, into each a special flavor,
some sweet, some bitter,
according to how much consumed
and what refused. Something similar in all, something Adirondack, though each, strangely different, yet, unmistakably alike, though, no bones of those close, buried or lost in this wilderness, when first they came. Many quick deaths

brought about the change.

"Come you now, Newcomer, whatever your breed, drink of this brew though diluted it be, drink of it to carry its name, in your blood, give you strength, and a love for the land, to do as you do where now you live, and here to stay until you're dead.

"What to call them, those who, in this land remote, stayed with seasons all, for years long, as if, here they belonged; as if, nowhere else they had, or now, cared to go. A name to fit them because of where they lived, and how they lived, and what they did to survive winter's wantonness. So little at the start, here where no others dared or cared to live: A name for all and for what they stood. A name more for men than for mountains.

"Many a winter they cried, save the dead till spring, open the womb of the earth, in graves deeply dug, drop extinguished life.

"Pick new blooms to set beside humble tombs, old or fresh.
Save the dead till spring when
petal-kissed faces bleed paths
of tears; sorrow incubated
in a sea of sterile snow
painfully set free.
Save the mourning till spring,
when smiles squeeze out gloom.
Glad again its spring,
glad new life to see,
glad to forget grief of winter.

Spring, from every open face, a happy grin.

"Settlers first, set the scene
beyond their day and generation.
Nothing changes that, nothing we say or do. Can't be any other way and stay Adirondack.
Those first always first,
The truth, hard and simple.

"Don't know if words more
I need so you understand.
Sometimes words too many,
too many times wrong.
What to say, when I do not know
what it is that should be said.

"A newcomer long you'll be
to those already here,
though numbers ever fewer.
Those who later come,
numbers ever increasing,
one day, a newcomer no more.

"Wherever I deliver in these
mountains, faces unfamiliar, dress
peculiar, yet, Adirondackers,
they say, are they.
Some, I wouldn't call by this name
if born and died here twice.
Others, I wish would just go;
others, polite and right.

"Some here one season,
Want to run the show, tell us,
All they know, all they've got,
all they want,
all that should be done,
say, of us, they are one.

Don't know if I like that.
Can't put outsiders in where
they don't belong and soon gone with the
promise of a fat paycheck.
With such telling and yelling
I'd like to tell them where to go,
when telling might do some good.

"If you're thinking of staying,
if the reason for coming here
is not just to take up space,
not just an escape from place,
forget most of what I just said.
Remember: being an Adirondacker
has nothing to do with
where you get your mail.
Here's your mail. See what I mean.

"A better way, out stay, out live
those already here when you first came.
No guarantee. Some live a hundred years
or more and outsiders still,
on the inside to their last breath.

"Mail light today. Time for talk.
My job is a lonely one; no partner with
whom to converse.
Always in a hurry to reach each box
on schedule as each place has set.
Only time I see some is when I'm late.
Today, you waited to say hello. I said,
I'll be a little late. Took time to
welcome you. Fast or slow, pays the
same: no more, no less.

"My name is Jake. I deliver six times
a week. A substitute delivers when I'm
off. If you're out of stamps just
leave cash with your outgoing mail.
Sometimes I take a break to fish or hunt

to remind me there's more to being an Adirondacker than delivering mail. I spoke more to myself than you. Am I only an Adirondacker by name? More to it than just being born here. I've been running this route for fifteen years. There's 450 boxes on my route. When I started it was half that, but you're the first that found me. Never have I spoken so much to one waiting for mail. It was good to get that off my chest. I'll be thinking much about what I said. Thanks"

"It's you I have to thank Jake," said Mr. Hill. "You set me straight. I won't forget what you said. But I have a word for you. All who come don't want to relinquish old ties. Living in the country is just that. Wherever it might be. Their identity is in where they came from not in what they have or have not become by living somewhere else.

"Some born on a mountain seek the lights of the city, and some born of city noise seek the quiet of the mountain. Of luck or misfortune, a coincidence of where one's born. Regardless of where we're born its an adjustment to circumstance and place, a slow evolutionary process of acceptance, rebellion or outright rejection. It's a process to stabilize shifting attitudes, restless adaptability and unfocused love. People want place. In a mobile society, place often means many places. Widespreading roots, not taproots. We're scattered, fragmented, physically and geographically, yet the inner self craves stability, identity and place. Need I say more?"

"I think you're right," said Jake shaking his large head in agreement, as he shifted to drop back into the truck. "I think you're right. Glad another Adirondacker is rooted on my route. Your attitude of place, I like. Glad you found yours." As the truck moved away, he waved and shouted, " Have a good day, John."

"So long," Jake.

HIGHWAY ADIRONDACKER

A highway Adirondacker am I.
It's the blacktop road for me,
A highway wide and smooth
Free of traffic jams.
A highway I ride
Through houseless hills.
No more woodland trails,
No more soggy, old logging-roads
With hardly room for two,
Side by side, to walk.

Now I ride highways here.
An airy flow in this wildland
Shuttles me where I want to go.
A gas pedal worn smooth.
The odometer count
Over 10,000 miles per year,
And seldom beyond the line.
A highway Adirondacker am I.

No more rocky summits do I climb,
No more mucky swamps trudged.
Backwoods roads I no longer seek.
What changed my mood?
Back roads too bumpy,
Sometimes too dusty or too muddy,
Too slow as I now go.

No views better than
What new, wide highways show.
Most any view, a view for heart.
Views to lure wanderers back,
Inspire residents to remain.
Panoramas unreeling,
Every mile, a clutter of scenes.

By a highway I live.
No place else I dare set my house
Live my life then where
The snowplow rides close.
A highway Adirondacker am I.

My roadside mail box
A frog's leap from my door;
Powerline poles stand
Strong and high nearby,
Not made useless
By fallen trees beaver cut.

I wish not to live each day
With uncertainty of light.
I want my electric there
To warm me, to enthrall me
With TV screen and voice,
To run a hundred things
I now admit I'd miss
Like a hot shower any hour.

A go-backer I am no more
With the Northway at my door.
No worry of roads ravaged
By play of summer winds
Or smothered by drifting snow.
A go-backer no more,
A highway Adirondacker I am for sure.

SPRING SNOW

What a fuzzy snow is this.
A cautious clipping
Of night's hoary beard,
Covers every surface and shape;
A gift from night to dawn,
A quick return with sun before noon.
Such a gallant quest
Of a disappointed guest
Again to claim what once its domain.
Ah, the cold delight stirs my soul.
A sight too pure to betray,
A last winter fling with spring.

SKIP'S CAMP

Your camp,
A frame of spruce poles
Gathered from a fallen forest,
Covered with thin canvas,
A shelter from rain,
Snow and cold.

Not a camp
On a point of land
For all to see and envy,
But hidden in the
Oswegatchie backlands
Where few cared to go.

A camp...
Only gotten to
By foot, by canoe
And time.

A camp...
That matched so well
The natural scene,
You were almost in it
Before you saw it.

A camp...
You lived for
Twelve months of the year;

A life...
Weaved around
A humble shelter
In the woods.

A camp...
So simple
Few could see an attraction,
Forgetting
Where it was
And why you went.

A camp...
Just right for two,
Three a crowd.

A camp...
A mattress on boards,
A tiny table,
Two folding chairs,
A narrow shelf,
A storage box,
A small boxstove
With a long, tin chimney pipe,
A plank floor.

On shoes of ash frames
And rawhide webs,
In quest of beaver pelts,
To this camp,
A refuge in the wilderness,
We trudged...
In the mid-night snow,
After the second shift
At the mine.

A camp...
A place of wild stillness;
A camp...
A palace with a friend.

A camp...
Less permanent
Than a beaver's hut,
A fox's den,
A squirrel's hole.
But it had to go, they said,
And with it went the woodsman.

A legal wilderness now, they say,
New laws outlaw camps.
A lovely wilderness, yes,
Where a visitor only is man;
A lonely wilderness, yes,
A home no more for woodsmen.

BOG RIVER FALLS

A summer late.
Why has it held back?
July, no desire to splash,
No voices at tumbling waters.
August, at last.
Wild with glee the young
Into deep pools plunge,
Shout in play
Too long held back.

Gangly boys on slippery rock slide.
Fun for others to watch.
Girls in shorts stare
A quick decision,
Bored with watching.
On a screaming note
Leap from a standing lot:
Slide the slippery chute,
A howling chorus of joy.
In happy protest
And reckless abandonment,
Bodies slide and collide
In pools of cool anonymity.

Who on the slick rock first to ride?
No one knows, no one cares to guess.
Surely none would suppose
Who would be the last.
Nature's game too long to ask.

"Take me," each leaper cries,
"I am a child again, a child of nature.
Tell me of the many rivers

That within me flow,
That distribute life,
That collect sediments of death."

This day, a river of play.
Cool water, invigorates life.
Shocks it, into living triumph,
Stirs the wild within.

Slick water runs black,
Broken water leaps white,
A cascade, black and white;
Water soft and flowing
Eternally working its art...
Sculpturing rock.

No beauty in the name..Bog.
A sour connotation.
Cranberries, pitcher plants
and tamaracks.
An acid drink, they like.
The Falls redeems
The Bog.

From a stony bridge people peek,
Fear to wet their feet.
Enough to see, no time to feel
What begs fulfillment
Where desire waits.

Again alone am I.
None stay as long. Why?

A reverie...
A river void of voices
Not its own,
A murmuring litany
A monologue of time
Uncounted.

A PEOPLE MOUNTAIN

Who cares
Why a little mountain
Southwest of Tupper
Is called Arab,
In this Adirondack land?

Who cares?
Climbers come
To be with a mountain,
Not with a name.

They come
To get on top
To look down
Instead of up?

Day-hikers come
By way of a narrow trail,
A climb steep but short;
The wide, circular view
Soon won.

Mountaineers call it,
A mountain with a long slant,
A child's stroll;
A mountain still
For those who come to look

From its open crown
What a sight of so much greenery
Unmarred.

On perfect days families come
In steady streams
Of legs, arms and screams;
Like bobbing corks
Pop to the summit
Turned playground.

Alone and in pairs,
In three and fours
In cheery groups
Of many more, they come.
Set voices free,
Shout into space,
A universe without end.

Lovers come
To sit and talk
With a mountain,
Kiss in the sun.

Children come,
With little hands
And laughing hearts,
Fill tiny palms
With cloud-caressed blueberries,
Firm and beady,
Big enough,
For stomachs small
And quickly satisfied.

They come,
With a kind wind,
When waxwings,
In flitty flight,
Skip among cherry branches,
As though, by fickle appetite,

Each limited to a cherry or two,
From every other tree.

The lonely come,
And sometimes
For hours sit,
When a mountain
Feels like a friend.

A comedy scene
Of rolling humps and heaps
An oddity of furrowed hills
Crowd this mountain;
Afar, mountains abrupt,
With ragged crowns, leap.

A geological gallery,
Each hump, each heap,
Like stilled waves
At rest,
A sleeping sea of trees.

A dream canoe set adrift
Over soft, leafy crests
Of maple, birch and popple.
Ride up, ride down,
Green swells of forested froth;
Cascade into glistening glens,
Along a fingered lake to the south,
Where hide houses and camps.

Find a mountain to climb,
Big or small, named or unnamed,
Makes no difference for a start.
Sit and wait upon a summit.
When it speaks you'll know,
No longer, are you,
A flat-lander Adirondacker,
With only a vision from below.

TAMARACK IN THE STOVE

Boisterously your bones protest
A jig of joy they dance
To flame and heat?
A lively response:

Snap...crack...snap...crack
With popping, flashing sparks.

Louder and louder with protest;
Hot and long, with flame.
Maybe more to celebrate.

A jubilant cry of release
From tight bark and stationary stem.
At last, at last skyward bound,
An exit of escape found.
At last, at last a journey
Long awaited to freely roam,
A new recourse now in space,
Alight again somewhere with life?

"At last a tamarack no more," it spoke.
In a final flame and whiff of smoke.

PAT DACY'S DEADLY SAW

A hundred years or more ago,
Lumberman Pat Dacy came
To these northern Adirondacks
From Michigan's chopped-up woods,
With a plan and a deed,
A 30,000 acre tract,
Tucked under his belt.

His plan: cut big, green trees,
As fast as he could instigate
Saucy crews of lumberjacks,
Frenchmen a-plenty from Quebec,
Some Swedes and Irishmen too.

His plan: 100,000 board feet per day,
Or more if he could keep the men,
To stay and cut from light to dark
To run the Brandon mill to make him rich
For pay as small as he dare give.

With his deadly cross-cut saw, Dacy came
The first seen here, they say,
One for each two of his special crews.
"There'll be no fellin' here," he said,
"With axes. The sharp saw is king now,
Straight cuts all I want,
With this long, two-man saw:
One rides while the other pulls
To make it sing as it should,

Cut spruce like cake and rake its dust.
I tell ya men, this saw is a must.
Too much wood chopped and left on the
Stump with a double-bitted axe.
Good for limbin' and notchin'
But that's about it."

A Frenchman named Oscar,
Did not agree with boss Dacy.
No partner would he be,
At the end of a cross-cut saw;
No one need pull him to work,
Not he, an axeman, a one-man show,
Who could fell and limb more spruce
Than any cross-cut crew.

"I'll not share my pay," he said,
"With one who rides while I pull.
No fool am I to fall for this new thing,
None of that for this Frenchman."

"Time ya learned, proud Frenchman,
To use the long saw," said Dacy,
"If it's work in these woods ya want;
If not, then to the mill go
And tell them it's there
You'd rather work for ya pay,
Then bending ya back as a lumberjack
Swishing a long, steel saw,
Cursing words a-plenty
Over whose holding back,
Free riding or out of track,
Teeth not traveling
As fast as they should.
Sharp teeth cleanly cut wood;
None to be out-done by the other one,
Each sure he's the best,
But none pass this Frenchman's test.
He's the best," he says.

The land now dismal
Where Dacy's crew rudely cut,
Now lays at rest, a long wait,
For trees of heritage to redress;
Soil too thin where fire raged
After the lumbermen left;
Charred stumps still remain,
Species kind---popple and birch,
Balsam and bracken work to heal and hide
This chastisement of land by man
And Dacy's...deadly cross-cut saw.

LIFE

ON THE LINE

A fur trapper...
He calls himself.
Creatures wild he catches
With traps cleverly devised.

Market for pelts
Good or almost nill,
There he'll be,
On the line.
Can hardly explain why,
To self or others.

To satisfy
A passion to kill?
For some innate thrill?
He's sure it's none of this
When in the forest deep,
Or wading a shallow marsh
Far from sight and sound,
Or there by a busy highway
Where he follows his line.

A measure of skill
Keeps him there,
But more an inner drive
That brings him back,
Year after year.
No reason to explain.

WET WOODS

Woods glow green,
Rain drenched and clean;
Too frequent, too dreary,
Air chilly, air damp,
Sitting in camp.

Put another log
On the fire,
Something to inspire
With smoke talk
And snappy response.

Woods glow green,
Rain drenched and mean,
Wait and see, please,
How long it takes
For rain to cease,
Sitting in camp.

Put another log
On the fire
Before we retire,
Let's see how long it takes
To sleep
With rain drops for dreams.

A WOODCUTTER'S LAMENT

"Logger by choice, stovewood cutter
By demand. Crooked culls,
Cores black and soft, grain stained,
Once left to rot.
Now in these hills,
Culls sell good as firewood
At twenty-five dollars
A sixteen inch face cord.
That's pretty good.

"Could get twice that in Syracuse,
Maybe three or four times more
Where there's not much real wood.
In stove and fireplace, though,
It's hard maple and yellow birch
You want for staying heat.

"When cool days chill,
Quick-fire aspen and snappy spruce,
And other dry, junk kindling
Will do.

"A different story
When winter decides its time
To crystallize and kill.
Then, dense, heavy wood you need,
The kind that grows slow and long,
And in a stove glows and throws heat,
That holds kindly to your bones.

"This simple truth I tell all
Who buy my wood."
With an added thought
He looked up from his
Still, chip-dusted chainsaw
And said, "Winter is not a time
For cheating people
But for keeping them warm."

"I'll take four cords cured,"
I said. "Can you make it five?
Loaded my truck takes ten.
Another order for five cords,
Up your way. Makes it easier
To calculate an even half."

"Make it five," I said.
"More will do us no harm
While less may not be enough."

"Be there Friday morning.
Any problem with that?"

"I'll flag a spot where to dump
In case I'm not here
When ya come."

What Friday he would deliver
He did not say. I presumed
He meant two days hence.
I was wrong. Several Fridays
Were spent before a disheveled pile
Of wood smothered the waiting flag.

The wood was split and dry and of
Species sought and said -- sure enough
But not a lot -- something short.
Not in pieces but in the look
Of the pile. Not big enough.
"Is that all of it?" I asked son Ken.
"That's it," he said.

I do not wish to question honesty
Or say something to offend, but,
I'm sure this pile is not half of ten.
Easy to measure stacked wood,
Easier yet, to make a miscalculation
A fact with proof.

"Was it five cords you left
Or less than that?" I asked
The woodcutter over the phone.
"Five it was," he said.

"The stacked wood does not
Agree," I said, with the hope
It would not cause a stir.

"What do you mean? Was the load
Short?" He asked with a voice
That left room for a mistake.

"Less than four, I counted,"
I said, but added, "Can't see
How your count went wrong.
Come and count the stacks
For yourself, four by eight to the inch."

"No need for that," he replied.
"Pay for what you got.
Though I sold ten cords
I'll get paid for less.
Some get more, some less,
Few stack to see what they've got.
Never called back to claim
An overload. Some think
I'm generous, others that I've
Held back. But its ten cords
In every load, whatever way it goes."

THE LAST

HOLDOUTS

Patches of snow in shadows still,
Grow smaller, grow smaller,
Minutes only torched by sun.
Ground mouth assimilating you.

Islands of white, once again ice,
Pressed hard with frost of night,
Slows the melt, slows the melt.

Patches of snow, the last holdouts,
Flags of truce, winter's last retreat,
Snow patches soon, no more in sight,
Then, for sure, it's safe
To say it's spring.

MOMENTS OF TRUST

Look at all the Canada geese,
Here in this public park
Where tasty weeds and rich grasses grow.

No one about while greedy geese
Search for generous handouts,
Wait for someone with children
And loaves of bread
And grain to scatter.
Around each picnic table
They mill as if people were there
Throwing things good to eat.

Around camping vehicles they step,
While occupants still sleep,
Or from a small window, watch
And wish, perhaps, upon wild geese,
Now and then, they could feast
Like a king of old with game a-plenty.

Gander and goose,
Yank grass and weed still green,
Safe from gun and almost anything.
This you seem to know,
None here to harm you.

Graze with ease,
But gaze suspiciously,
Yet when a hand held out,
Come close and stretch
A long black neck,
To get what is offered.

A strange trust without knowing why.
Someplace else, a wild creature yet,
Where trust evaporates,
Where fear commands frantic flight,
A loud, alarming retreat.

FOREST RANGER

An outdoor career most dear,
For some, without regrets,
No change from year to year.

A job on the payroll of the State
To put forest fires out,
Lost persons, seek and find.
With one, adequate equipment a sure win,
With rain, the best tool against wind.
With the other, who can tell
Whether a search ends
In heaven or hell.

A job that rides a lot with hope,
Hope to prevent and hope to find.

Rangers in green, seldom seen,
Soon on the forest scene
When an open fire goes wild
Or a mother cries, Find my child."

BY WHAT FIRE DO YOU SIT?

Adirondacker...
Tell me, if you can,
What is this controversial debate
In your part of the state
Really about?

I see much smoke arising
From many camps where voices shout
Conflicting words about the same land;
Which to believe, which to doubt,
Which to finally put out.

Hearts different in shape and beat?
In which camp rests the true you?
Can you tell by the fire
And the wood that burns there?
Can you tell by the sound of the voices
And the words spoken?

Each fire warms,
Each voice says its true,
Yet how are you to know for sure,
By what fire you should sit,
And to what voices you should listen
And join in the cause?

Each a flag of a different color, waves.
There's a red and there's a blue,

There's a brown and a green too,
There's a white,
A purple and a black here.
What message each unfurls?
Color and cause match each group.
This you ask:
Which speaks for you
Which for itself?

What is the common cause
Without deliberate exaggeration,
Without postulating
To make a vague point seem right?

By whose definition, the common cause?
Which for the Adirondacks
And which for the Adirondacker?
Can it be so divided
And remain a just cause?
Which under the guise of either
Works best for itself?
Which is incensed with condemnation
Without just examination
Of causes and reasons beyond their own?
Which rails dictatorial methods of one
Only to replace them with their own
Dictatorial demands?

Adirondacker...
What words do you best understand?
Under what flag can you stand
And know it is the true one
For you and the land?

Is the flapping flag with the big "W"
A symbol for wildness,
A symbol for pure water,
A symbol for meaningful work,
Or for wanton wreckage
In the battle to win

A land-use war?

A "W" in reverse, a capital "M"...
Is this for mountains wild and many,
Or for mountains making money,
Flashing, twinkling lights,
Advertising commercialized command,
Where the buck rules the land?

Adirondacker...
We have much raw land unexploited yet,
A sense of frontier still,
Not homesteads for newly weds
With a dream to claim and tame,
That frontier long dead.

The frontier now
Big timber companies moving out,
Huge estates on the market or soon,
The rich relinquishing lands,
Few have seen and walked
Outside of family or club.
Others aspire to acquire this land,
To fit a financial scheme.

Room for you, Adirondacker?
This you may think they mean,
Just a game of changing locks
From one or two, to quite a few?
No new frontier for you.

Of what use, big lands set free
Swallowed up by the state?
Better all to claim a wild domain;
Without apology
A wilderness by demand.
Resist not this change of heart
And how a land against the world
Now stands as an entity of peace.

ORPHAN LAND

Mother dead, while in her arms still,
Words never uttered
So she could hear what I said;
Gone she, before I spoke,
Father too, soon dead.
Years enough only: an image, a voice,
A face to remember.

Neither knew what it was
To long be wed.
Two sons too young
To know the damage deep,
What lasting harm done,
To heart, soul and attitude
Spread through years of yearning.
Hearts tightly sealed within,
A sure defense to hide a hurt
Unknown; windows slightly open,
Ready at the door to unlock,
Come a gentle loving knock.

Orphans too long, too long denied
Embraces and kisses of love
With happy laughter displayed.
So young, by hornets of death stung,
Neither knew what each sting meant
Or where a poison finally set.

With a wife to this land I came
With a dream and a life
Each to unravel and decipher;
A web of roots to plant

In soil too shallow, perhaps,
To hold with growth and years.

One only lingers now,
With a dream still.
No place here for those who,
By choice gone, no dream to stay.
Orphan more with years,
Even to one's own alive.

BARK

NOT FOR ME

Call me, barkeater no more,
A name of centuries gone,
A people who, on mud soup
Of tree bark and bud.
Winter storm and cold
Survived.

Adirondacker...
Barkeater......
No longer brother names.

Adirondack...
A name of today,
A name of new birth,
A name of a beautiful land.
Barkeater now a meaningless name,
Unless of mud soups you drink.

Venison eater, beaver eater,
Rabbit eater, partiridge eater...
Yes...yes...yes...yes
Barkeater...no.

Barkeaters, lowly rodents:
Beaver, porcupine, muskrat and rabbit,
Better their flesh to eat
Than bark of aspen, hemlock and birch;
They make more of it than we.

HERE NO MORE

Gone South, the family,
A one-way flow from the North.
Gone where seldom flies the snow;
Gone where the land is flat,
A long finger into the sea;
Gone where sun shines long and bright;
Gone where thunder and flashing light
Comes with clouds so slight.
Nothing here in the North
To bring them back.
Gone the family,
Gone South
For good.

BRIDGES GONE

Adirondacker...
How we rush to erase what others built.
Gone now, many of our girder bridges,
Too soon condemned whether good or not.
Winter and rain tough on steel.
"Salt baths hasten the end,"
Say inspectors of the State.

Not a word of opposition met,
Nor a notice of regret...
At the passing of girder bridges:
Superstructures of solid steel
With canopies most impressive;
Giant box-trap cages,
Nothing ever caught:
No tripping devices,
Slamming gates,
An opening at each end.

Gone first toy-like structures
Spanning brooks, narrow streams.
Gone now where rivers run wide.
Gone from the Saranac and the Sacandaga
And others too, while a few,
A last repair.

How we rush to erase what others built
Though many still remember when
Vehicles first rumbled across
Stretching trusses of painted steel.

Each generation dictates its right
For its style of room and speed
As though a reason beyond need.
A desire for doing
And of changing scene.

Beam by beam, bones of steel,
Beam by beam to wrench, torch
And crane, angular arches
Soon succumb. None morn a dream
Dismantled, a bridge of short glory.
A utilitarian design reduced
To shaky stacks.

This gray day over one such bridge,
Straddled by its archless replacement,
I pass, a last passing. Gone---when
Again I come this way.

Gone from the scene of the Raquette
All trace of rusted old steel.
Here now, a primitive, uncluttered span,
No more play with big-boy Erector sets
To exhibit engineering designs
To complicate the measure of stress
For transporting, by wheel and speed,
Tonnage over space
And what it takes to make it safe.

Look at its severe replacement,
No web of mighty steel on display,
Nothing overhead, low rails only,
Nothing to clutch a monster truck
Gone berserk.

Gone most of our girder bridges
With canopies most impressive,
A never yielding net to stall
Leaping rages of speed.

Ride now a rigid, smooth back
Of herculean steel laid flat.
Better here concentrate strength
Then with slanting girders
And connecting braces
Enclosing space.

How we rush to erase what others built.
How we pride the bridge at Jay,
Protest its removal: say, let it stay
Why do we hold to one covered with wood
And let bridges of steel go,
So ungrudgingly.

Yes, many of our girder bridges gone,
Too soon condemned whether good or not;
Winter and rain, tough on steel.
"Salt baths hasten the end,"
Say inspectors of the State.

BROTHER WINTERS

At last, a big snow:
Not a warning, not a tease;
Not a legion of crystals
Lost in a bitter breeze,
A sky of fallen moon moss,
Lifeless wherever it alights?

A year ago, a winter
Too wintery, too early,
Too soon at every door,
A white, dense fence stood,
To hold in what it could.

Those who dare not challenge
Cold and snow stayed within
As if to avoid indulgence
In some great sin.

None could hold in
Those who look long,
And see no sin in snow
Deep and pure,
Would not stay within,
Ventured far, an arctic heaven
Of angel hair and flowing gowns
A mask of a hundred demons of doom.

This year winter late,
Late by weeks:
Not a glacial monster
With long claws of ice
Clutching every house;
Not a ruthless lover
With a smothering embrace.
A year hence, what a difference:
A winter almost kind,
With no design to trap and confine.
Look now, has it changed its mind?

APPLES

OF AUTUMN

Apples wild, apples wild,
Picked from a tree or two,
Hidden where few know they grow
And fewer still who care to taste.

Deer know when to come and feast
On apples fallen or at easy reach.
When a craving says,
Those higher are better,
A deer soon decides to try,
With forelegs lifted and neck extended,
To snatch, with pointed mouth,
A special apple, high on a naked bough,
That like a Christmas ornament hangs,
Waiting for a gusty wind
To whip it from its grip,
And from its pedicel plummet
To a grassy or snowy pouch below.

Apples wild, apples wild,
Late in season,
Apple flesh left too long
On ground and limb,
Tempts a prowling, hungry bear
With a passion for apples,
Wild and sour,
Skin bags of cider fermented.
This the reason for the glut?
Bear, go easy on the tree,
Remember, each year,
You'll want apples a-plenty.

Bear, you're dizzy already,
Better you bivouac this night
Under an apple tree.

Take this word, as true, dear friend,
Many of your kind stagger
Into an ignoble path of death
When done in by an apple glut:
By baited pile or an abandoned tree.
Done in by gun or bow.
And if you're too slow
It's by the highway demons you go.

Bear, you apple drunk,
Go to sleep and dream deep,
Dream of tomorrow and apples more.

APRIL SNOW

Call it sugar snow
Not for reasons shared
By those who tap
Hard maples for sap,
Boil to syrup,
Even sugar, perhaps.

This sprinkling
On a crumb cake earth.
A temporary display,
A winter scene in play, perhaps.

Already a bright early sun
Says goodbye to a vanishing pelt,
As robins appear with the melt.

Snow minus its sting...
A warm April spring,
A strange delight,
A pleasant light,
Nothing to fight,
A battle won?

SWIVELED THRONE

You Adirondacker...
With scissor and comb in hand,
It's woods and hills you roam,
Guided by those seated and gowned
On your swiveled throne.

Questions many point the way:
Climb mountains high,
Paddle rivers long;
Catch trout and shoot deer;
Experiences varied, converted soon,
Fragment by fragment, to opinion:
Strongly voiced and easily changed,
Customer by customer, day by day.

In crops of hair, thick and thin,
You thrash the brush and part the swale;
In the safety of your tiny shop,
You know all hardships, all dangers,
Been the poacher and the game cop,
To right a wrong in the night.

You Adirondacker...
With scissor and comb as you stand,
What you learned of the land
You learned with scissor in hand
From those who sit
Upon your swiveled throne.

BROTHER BE GONE!

Good brother, now years
In the dark you rest.
Near and dear have you been
In your waiting, as though
Waiting for me to journey
With you into the dark.

Heavy the burden
To harbor the grief
Of two hearts in one:
One in the dark of final freedom
Yet reluctant to go;
One still in the light
Refusing yet to yield,
Searching instead,
With life and love,
A hand to hold,
A heart to know and trust,
In the light and in the dark.

Good brother, take leave.
Much you've given me
To live life through
But let the grief be gone,
Let life go on.

An appointment we'll keep
When my time is done.
See you then.

MR.

THE DEER HUNTER

Adirondacker...
With flame and fall of leaves:
September red, October gold,
November brown,
A hunter's heart afire.

Not for beauty of leaf,
But final goodbye of foliage,
A stalking heart awaits.

In naked November woods,
Pointed tines, a polished rack,
A crown of rank, a right to reign
As a kindred king
Within its range of duty.

Genders' ancient role:
Genes set rigid rules,
Genes against genes.

A buck adorned...
Lunges for quick escape.
Too late, too late.
Boom! A bullet stops
What bone it strikes.
A mission done, a hunter won.

Such a dream is yours?

VENISON GETS THE DEER

Your success baffles all.
You tell them again and again,
Deer know you as if one of their kind
Because venison runs wild in your veins.

You say, since you were a child,
Venison you ate, and your appetite for it
Never ceases, even increases.
This is why you're sure deer come close
Though a last mistake.

Your simple philosophy:
The more venison you eat
The more deer you're bound to meet.

The cycle continues, year after year,
When asked how you do it you laugh.
Some say you're just a man of luck;
Others say you just know the right spots.
Sure there's more to it
Than that, more to shooting big bucks
Way back in the Adirondacks than luck
And knowing where to go.

You smile and let them think a while.
Then you remind them again:
Eat more venison and a real hunter
One day you'll be. Some fresh flanks
You offer and they say:
We'll get our venison by the gun.

You tell them again, venison is all you
Need. Doesn't matter where you get it
As long as you eat it.
It drives a hunter on.
Demands he wait for hours,
Whatever the weather,
Standing as still
And as quiet as a tree.

Others claim
Deer you lure with a wink.
You know this isn't true, unless
There's need for meat in camp and
A deer is near. Sometimes it's hard
To shoot when you want a big one
And a mini-rack appears.
What luck is that if you take it?
Maybe, you forget to fill out your tag.

Maybe you've heard this
Old Adirondack story
For some getting so much more,
And some getting so much less or none.
Believe me, listen to what he says,
It's venison that gets the buck,
Venison running in a hunter's blood,
Not bullets in the gun.

Still, few acknowledge the secret,
And turn to gadgets and gimmicks
To change their luck from bad to good.
If only they could, they would.

Again they ask, what's the trick?
No trick, no holding back, you say.
Eat more venison, all you can get.
Make sure it's fresh for no regrets.
A venison sandwich on watch sure helps.

Quick - give me some of that Venison!

This, the real test, you'll soon see.
Wherever you go, buck and doe
Look you up,
Blow a curious hello.
That's your clue to do what you must
If venison you want in your blood.

I'll tell you one better, he said,
Venison stays long in the blood.
Who would believe it stays
Until its deadly mission,
Of deer against deer,
Is complete.
Not 'til a deer lays dead
At the hunter's feet does it end.
But with a venison feast
It begins all over again.

You see,
It's not the gun, not the man
That gets the hunted buck,
But venison running wild in one's blood.

SUMMER GONE

Suddenly September,
Suddenly low, dreary clouds;
Too cool, too fast,
Too ominous to last.
Has summer really gone?

Suddenly September dark.
A ghost only is summer,
A time of gloom too soon.

Summer spirits not yet dead.
Not through with long days
And short nights.

Suddenly September bright
Rescued by arborial splendor.
Now garlands of foliage
A-glow as though a-bloom:
Birch, ash and maple
Bleed yellow, orange and red.
Now gone, the monotony of green.

Hello, autumn splendor
As September ends.

SO MUCH SNOW

Snow * Snow * Snow *
I know, I know, I know,
It comes, it goes;
Snow * Snow * Snow *
It comes, it goes, it goes.

It comes in storms
Of sterile whiteness;
It comes silently
And hides away
What drabness it finds
And touches.

Snow * Snow * Snow *
Clouds of crystalline dust
Afloat in frigid air;
The fleece of frost,
Puffs of winter's breath
To set the old stage
With costumes quickly made.

Like feather croppings,
Like meal from a mill
Thrown to the wind,
It comes.

Leafy flakes so many,
Sculpture designs,
Intricate yet simple,
Soon wherever one looks,
Already said
In a thousand books.

Snow * Snow * Snow *
I know, I know, I know,
It comes, it goes,
I know, snow never wins.

A RIVER WILD

Come now, to the river,
The wild, wild river;
River far from roads,
River as of old.

Come now, come now,
Come now, while you may,
Come now, before the day,
A river wild no more.

Wild river at play,
Is yours, is mine;
Long river of silent time,
Is yours, is mine.

WHAT PEACE IS THIS?

So suddenly
My tranquility fractured,
Corrupted and dispelled
In a terror of torment
That questions the calm
Of selfish peace.

The futility of it
While hordes, far and near,
Suffer the humiliation
Of misery I know not;
From day to day, night to night,
Tremble with each moment
As though it were their last.
Better that, say some
Than hopeless entanglements
With circumstances tragic.

So many
In traps of satanic tyrants
Because of where they live,
What they believe
And how regarded
By powers against which
They are powerless.

Can I luxuriate in my peace,
Selfishly absorb it;
Saturate myself with it
As though meant only for one
Removed from the strife and the woe
Of a world beyond this tiny sphere?

Can I easily forget those unrightly
Denied what is mine?
Let the starving starve and soon die
On continents far?
Let the sick get sicker and soon die
Because none are here for me to see?
Can this a worthy peace be?

Is it not more
Than scene serene
And sound so sweet;
More than place ideal?
How can it be in a world
Where it is said: saints and sinners
Suffer alike.

GIVE US OUR SONG

Adirondacker...
Balladeer of the mountains
Search our hearts and the land
In quest of a song
That will stay
On lips of those who play
And those who sing of this land.

You balladeer with a small band
Or standing alone,
Guitar in hand,
Fingers strumming strings
As your songs you sing.
Leap into the pond of memories;
Through countless pages
Of words and pictures look;
Talk with friends old and strangers new,
Of time, of people, places and things.
Find that song for which we long.

Tradition hard to find?
Intuition takes its turn,
What to touch, what to preserve,
What to create in your song.

Adirondack balladeer
Give us a song immortal,
Not to store on museum shelves,
Not one few hear.
Put your song on the lips of all,
A joyful, robust anthem
That rings as clear in heart
As in words and voice.

We wait for our song,
A song that lives on.
Find it, release it,
Give it to us all.
Is that too much to ask,
Too great a task?
Adirondack balladeer,
Give us our song.

GOODBYE SWEET BLISS

I'm out for quiet
Where surroundings cooperate,
Not stillness of nature
But stillness of man.

Leaves blow in the wind,
A song of silence
We know.

Prattle of water
Against the hull
Of a motorless craft,
Sweet to hear.

Excited quacking, mallards
Taking sudden leave,
A homely song unchanged,
We cherish.

Old santuary of silence...
Space...sky space
Now penetrated by man's
Flight
A thunder. a roar
Through silences of space.

Woes of heaven...
No storm in sight.
A speck, a streak
Of white on blue
Throws back a path,
A collision of sound;
An earth bouncing boom
Foreshadows a mission of doom.

Has earth come to this:
No room for quiet...
Goodbye sweet bliss.

THE DISTANT SCENE

Adirondacker...
What you see from your street
Is what you know best as Adirondack.
Always a far scene, never too close
To what is wild and rough,
The distant scene enough.

The weather you need not seek,
It seeks you instead.
Adirondack, a land you love,
From day to day, ask nothing
But from a window each morn to gaze
Upon this land as though
A colossal mural easily seen,
Always grand, always there.

And from a familiar road
You daily travel
This beauty viewed
As on a giant movie screen.
A love that takes without taking;
A love that gives without giving,
Each a sweet compromise
With tender surprise.

So you think yourself
More an Adirondack lover
Than an Adirondacker.

Who best loves,
Those enveloped by what they love
Or those who preserve distance
And prospective?
None can tell,
None can tell,
But those who love,
But those who love
And know, what is love,
And know, they love.

Adirondacker, where you live
Makes no difference
If from there you love
This land, this land Adirondack.

A SURE MEAL

High in a hardwood
A hawk stiffly stalks,
Eyes piercing, stares at
The slaughter slab;
A meal table today
For hawks headed north;
By wheel and bumper
A sure-catch counter.

Hawks perch here
Along a noisy Northway,
An easy swoop,
A quick lunch stop,
No time to hunt while on the go.

Now, a hovering hawk
Anxiously waits
For a chance to steal
Prey killed by wheels
Without appetite.

Look here,
Already a burgered rabbit
Lays on a warm, asphalt plate.
Needs some pulling
And some shaking
For the taking.

All yours hawk!
Don't take your eyes
Off the road though,
Or like your prey
You'll soon there lay.

THERE GOES JIM

From our kitchen window,
A private little show
Of a long-tailed performer
We have learned to know.

We call him Jim of the limb.
His coat now thick and dim,
With winter already too near,
He prepares for it without fear.

This day, pine cones his feed.
We confess, he works a great deal
To uncover each hidden seed.
We wonder, how many make a meal?

We like to think he knows,
We stop to watch his shows,
That he wants us to look
And see, he needs no cook.

FLOYD GILMORE

Floyd was a drinking man
Without any doubt.
But there was more by far
To him than a sudden bout
Now and then,
At a Saranac or Placid bar.

First an Adirondack woodsman,
A woodsman as of old,
With few to compare,
As all friends attest
Who have stayed at his rustic camp
Of sagging logs that sat high
In the sky on a little mountain
South of Averyville
Where a town road ends
At a farmer's yard.

This, his woodsman's paradise,
A paradise he proudly shared
Until the state crew came
To execute its nefarious task.
Charred timbers and ash, when done.
Floyd laughed to hide his hurt
And said, many a good year there,
What more could an old woodsman ask.

Wherever among the stars, he rests
In his camp at a place more sacred
Than that precious alpine acre
On which it once stood.

What more could an old woodsman ask?

BATTLE AT THE BAR

Adirondacker...
You, owner of this small bar,
A night tender of bottles and glasses,
A smiling server of beverages and liquors
That spark angels and bedevil demons?

Are you a seeker of fish and game by day,
Or have you put all this away as play?

The names of all your steadies you know
At a glance or a mere utterance.
You hear the contrived stories many,
A flow of words sometimes wise,
Sometimes so real you listen,
Before words, blurred and slurred,
Tainted with drink and time,
You listen no more.

Over your shiny, mahogany bar,
Stories Adirondack many
About people, about things
Not too far, sometimes too near.
Here, leaning over this open span,
For all to see, they stand,
Strong in word while glass in hand,
Like a deadly saber of honor
They dare not flash when sober.
Here a battle of hate afire,
Words fuming with self-betrayal,
Fists randomly flung at the nearest one,
Tongues twisted and eager to condemn
With a lampooning litany of names,

Claims against an enemy invisible.
A battle won by none.
At the door angry words die
Like flags without a demanding wind.

Adirondack battle, the prattle over land,
Left as is or by some other plan.
A battle not of guns and blood,
Not of foreign spirits for revenge,
But of neighbors, coalitions, committees
Councils, agencies, conservancies and...
Bureaucracies.
Who of these true lovers of the land?
A vision in reverse,
A right to one, a wrong to another,
By chance, change or calculated gain.

Adirondacker...barkeeper...
Does the park, does the land,
BELONG TO THE PEOPLE OF THE STATE?
What do you tell your clientele
To keep them at the bar
Or send them afar?

GONE

What more to say
That says it better:
Another dear friend gone,
Not just from sight,
But from the spectacle of life.

What seems strange, with
Parting and ceremony,
A sense of exception,
Death an uncommon commodity
Among those of promised immortality.

Another friend gone.
Near or distant, dear or acquaintance
Matters not, a vivid reminder:
What friend last before your call.

DEVOTED DUTY

Barbed wire...
Fence posts one after another,
A line trying to be straight,
Closest which, those right,
Or those left,
Or those that dance free
Upon wire strands that hold tight
To surviving posts attached yet,
Where they stand in soil?

Rusted, low wire
Through these woods run
Like a slinking enemy,
Not informed their job done.
No need now to inflict injury
Against anything wild or tame
That may come by.

Generations ago erected
To hold something in or out,
Not sure what most,
Man, cattle or other things.

Pasture no more, cattle no more,
Fences once so long, so fierce,
Yet so easy to erect,
Like a mania appeared,
One strand or two might do,
Three or four to make sure.

Pasture gone, forest now,
Bark embraced wire,
Steel barbs clutched by fleshy wood,
A living post, an indefinite enlistment,
Prolongs its task with time
As long as rust and wind and tree,
Let it last as a fence.

Barbed wire...
Hidden in the brush,

Stapled there a hundred years ago,
Where now I search and rush
To find an old boundary line.
Barbed wire won't neglect its duty,
Let me know its there,
Be it at rest or stretched;
Let me know it hasn't surrendered,
But simply waiting to do
What put there to do.
Though now, rough and flaked
With rust, these twisted points,
Still long, still sharp enough,
More a menace with rot,
Wait yet, in the name of a cause
To tear cloth and hide,
Without hesitation, penetrate flesh.
A cruel deed, of blood and pain,
To justify the long, patient vigil
Of a fossilized fence.

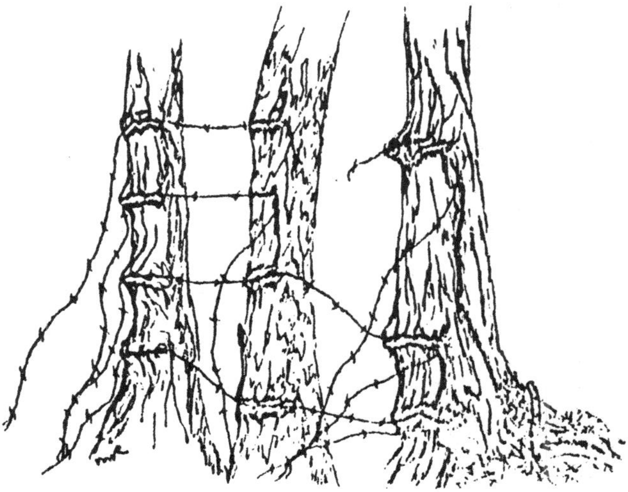

PATHS UNPAVED

Adirondacker...
Walk not just these paths
At your door.
Go also to untrodden ways,
Places still and wild
Where so infrequently tread
Gentle feet, voices sweet heard
In soft speech with whispering leaves
And fleeting wings.

Take to these woods
Unarmed with gun or rod,
Camera, palette or pen.
Go as though a fresh discovery,
An old friendship renewed.

Find that grassy meandering road
Long abandoned by county economy.
Now an asset, cherished and hidden,
Hugged by scarfs of disheveled trees.

These woods few care about
Too unkept, a sylvan shamble,
Nature in transition
Scrubby disarray to forest order.
No spectacular views,
No cool lodge and fast-food
Restaurant for fast retreat.

A walk without boot miles to count.
For moments tenderly spent afoot,
Ticking time forgot.
As if eternity touched.

HERMIT FATHER

Come my children...
Daughters three, sons four;
Too many hundreds of days,
None at my door.

How long must I wait:
Months, years, decades
Before one, two, three or all
Stand at my door?

How long must I wait
Before my end I reach,
No longer there
To meet them at the door?

With children...
Surely some there'll be
To play wildly about
With gleeful shouts of joy.

One day only some,
Or one day all,
A sudden curiosity,
A nagging obligation,
A calling answered
While here I am still
To meet them at the door.

One day never...
All at my door.

FOR THE LOVE
OF AN APPLE TREE

"Don't you fellas touch that apple tree," bellowed the old farmer leaning hard on his cane.

There he stood, at the door
of his weathered shed, an
extension to a tiny trailer,
a humble, solitary last home.

At the edge of his lot,
a brushing crew at work,
without notice or permission,
cutting fast with roaring machines.

Waving a stout stick
he shouted, again and again.
What chance had he to compete?

An angry monarch was he, a castle
in spirit he once ruled,
a house of laughing children.
A gift for them---an apple tree he
grew.

Sits he now, guardian of his property.
All gone, near and far, but the tree.

"Those upper limbs too close to the powerline. Won't cut more than we have to," shouted a young, husky foreman with a smile as if a guarantee of trust.

What care he, a brush cutter,
about an old apple tree, this
trailer king thought as he watched
from his rustic balcony.

"Them limbs ain't anywhere near your line. You know these trees ain't for growin' tall. Besides, this tree was here long before ya line, here before the kids were born, more than sixty years here."

"Just wanta be sure lines are clear, in case of a storm. It's our job for the pay we get. Old man, we'll go easy on your tree."

As chainsaws ripped flesh and bone
of trees and brush, He listened:
a promise hushed and crushed with
noise.

"As it stands, you know, it's a perfect apple tree. What will it be when ya men finish butcherin' it?"

"Sure your boss comes first. It's not your job to satisfy me. Ain't too much to ask: Have a little pity for this dear old tree and for me."

"You can count on us," said the foreman as he walked back to his crew.

"Hope so," said the old man as he turned from the cold.

With the slam of the door a traitorous foreman shouted, "Cut that damn tree so its no trouble to the line."

"I'll cut it at the fork on the side of the line," said a waiting cutter. "Better half a tree than none."

A promise heard; a promise
remembered.

"Cut it," said the foreman.

In seconds, the nasty deed done.
A hollow thud, a husky limb
sprawled beside a standing amputee.

"What have ya done out there," cries a familiar, thundering voice. "You damn fools, you liars. You said you would go easy on my tree. It's more than a tree to me. It's the memory of my children climbin' it, sittin' in it, callin' to me and their Ma, callin' to each other, cradled there, smilin' and smellin' sweet blossoms. That tree was heaven in spring with buzzin' bees too busy packin' pollin' to sting anyone. I couldn't hav' givin' them kids anythin' better then that apple tree."

The crew cringed...

"Who cares about cuttin' brush? Something different when its a tree someone cares about."

"Get off my land," roared the farmer. "Just another apple tree too close to the road and the line. No need for anymore cuttin.' My shotgun's by the door, and its loaded."

The father meant what he said, a threat of some legal consequence, a hurt too deep to care.

What would his daughter say, when her childhood tree she gazed upon, a tree mutilated, half standing, half on the ground as though severed by a tyrant's sword?

When at last she came and saw with eyes of disbelief, to the dear tree she ran as though to an injured child, and, caressing leafy branches, cried.

Again she came and knocked on her father's shaky door. Though she did not say why again she came, he knew it was for the tree. With leaf to lips, she sat and said:

"They'll not chip it into a million tiny pieces to rot beside the road. I'll make more of it than that."

With paternal approval he nodded.

"Cut it into 12 inch sticks," she said to her man-son.

In a cloud of blue-gray smoke, he triggered the chainsaw and cut the cherished limb.

To her heart she said:

"In my stove these sacred sticks I'll burn. The dreams they hold will come back to me as a last place to hide."

Then to her father, she said:

"My life lived. No other tree can I love.

He said in reply:

"I fought for the tree, more for you than for me or the tree. No other can we love, so long and dear."

ADIRONDACKER

Adirondacker...
Yes, a breed that chooses to live
Far from big cities,
Out of sight of them, at least;
Not reluctant to scorn places
Where too many people live.

City people say,
Hey man, how can you live there
Twelve months of the year;
Pleasant in summer
To escape city heat,
What a pity to live there all year.
Why live so far from everything,
From everything a city offers?

You say, why be where everything is
When everything no one can have.
For some, perhaps, there's more,
Not in accumulation,
In wanting, in demanding,
But in concentration
On who one is and what one has;
Not what's bought, or wrongly sought,
Not what one has not
Or where one lives,
Or where one dies.
For some, a clearer view
When free from crowds.
Among the trees we live
And the silence of a backroad,
A lakeside tourists abandon so soon.
A hamlet with one store, one church.
This the reason, perhaps,
Why some do not stay.
Silence stings the heart of
Those who fail to listen.

Adirondacker...
What do you want of this land?
You think of yourself as unique,
With a heritage, grand and wild,
When with the rest of the state compared,
So proud of the distinction
Then in another mood say, let us be
Like the rest of the state,
Forgetting perhaps,
How much of the state looks, and sounds
And smells to your dismay.
So maybe this is why you're here
And why you stay by the fire wild.

THE RIVER OUT FRONT

As my
Oswegatchie flows by,
It shows,
It knows
Its way to its sea.

Listen
As it goes
Gurgling
On its way.

Rolling, turning,
Bouncing, and sliding,
At this stage,
A river
Proud to be a river,
A young river,
A searching river.

At every age,
At every stage,
A river
Beautiful.

A river
That sings
Where few listen.

A river
That performs
Its daily dramatics
Without applause.

So I listen
And let its fresh waters
Flow through me
Like a gentle stream

Of liquid memories
From which I drink
When the heart thirsts.

Flowing river,
Ever growing
Smoother and wider,
Moving
Ever closer,
Ever closer
To its sea.

Far beyond
Where I watch,
A river
Tired of being a river.

But look here,
It gurgles and splashes
Gleefully,
And over here,
It mumbles and whispers
Mournfully.

Just ahead,
It tosses and lashes
Playfully and wildly
With turbulence and rage
Demonstrating a will
For mingling and creating
MANY STRANGE MOODS
Of terrifying tranquility.

Such it is,
For a river
On an endless journey
To its ever-waiting sea.

The envy of man,
The eternal intimacy
Of a river
With its sea.

THE BACKROADS RIDER

Adirondacker...
Rider and driver
Of back country roads,
Skeletal woods roads bare
Of the black skin
Of asphalt. You lover
Of swelling, dipping passages.

Backroad seeker,
Where pavement ends
A new time begins;
A reminder of when roads
Were gravel and dirt.
Wish no return.

Roads of tortuous irregularity,
A delight to drive and ride
When the spirit is right.
No need for speed
On roads unpaved.

Roads that roll and curve,
That meander and play
With the patience of drivers
In a hurry to get somewhere.
We miss much when we rush
On backwoods roads.

Backroad seeker,
Travel with a watchful eye,
Ready for quick glimpses
Of things wild.

No flatscapes,
No checkerboard roads
For you.
Wait and watch
As you drive on roads unpaved.
It's the way to go.

DEAR GUESTS

When in woods you live,
Your guests and company,
No formal invitation
No great preparation,
Out of nowhere, unannounced
Do they come and dally
In the yard.

Without apparent fear
They stand about
Waiting for you to come out
And welcome them in some special way
Just because they're deer.

Each with large bulging ears,
Pointed, erect, sometimes horizontal,
Just depends upon what is heard;
Sometimes each ear reaches forward
As though straining, not sure
Of what it hears.

Each high-held head, a defensive trio
Of sound and sight and smell;
An isosceles triangle of instinct,
To direct and protect its charge,
Each tells where to venture and not.
Yet here, deer come most any day,
More, perhaps, at night or early morn,
As new tracks reveal. I presume,
There's room for contradiction
In its head so flat on top,
For what is safe and what is not.

Sometimes in my haste, I dash
From the door, with eyes set low
And mind in thought, I almost
Bump into a waiting guest
Who does not step aside,
As if it wanted us to collide
So I would know it's there.

It's then that I stop and stare
And smile at the gangling figure
That stares back inquisitively
Not in surprise that I am here,
But that I have taken so long
To show and say hello.

Here it waits for words familiar
To complete its triangle of defense,
Identify a friend. Not satisfied
It stops again to stare,
As if to say, if you care,
Come closer.

When a glance tells its time,
I advance, a step or two,
Or, sometimes quite a few,
But not too many or too fast
To upset the delicate plan.

To deer, I talk as friends,
Not a one-way exchange.
Frequent flicks of raised ears,
Suggestive movements tell,
These words ring sweetly in its cranium.
Does this mean we mutually comprehend
As friends or must I confess, deer
Come more to see what treat
There is to eat
Than to converse with me?

Is it an apple you want, my deer?
If you'll wait, I'll fetch one bought;
Many now I cannot spare
As later in season, when bushels
I may pick to make big pots of lusty sauce.

When the cooking begins, then,
You'll come looking and whiffing
For juicy wild apples,
Though hard and sour to most,
Deliciously tart to you, and so right
For grasping and mashing
Like a cider press
In your long, narrow mouth.

Now, another here, not so inclined
To welcome, as I do, a deer friend,
A reason quite understandable, I guess,
For a young hound, mostly beagle:
No fault of his for being what he is.

Sometimes through a visit he sleeps,
As in a whisper I talk,
To a deer very near; but when
Wet nostrils catch the scent,
It matters not what he did not hear.
A bugle blast, loud and defiant,
He sends forth, a challenge,
I suppose, to my deer,
A way to make it run from a chase,
Without regard to friendship,
A kind his not to understand,
But likes instead, to end.

One after another, resound
Stout bellows for freedom,
Each accompanied by frantic lunges
Which rudely remind the hound
Of the limits of the chain.

Free it is not
On a wild hunting spree to run.

An innocent-faced guest, unruffled,
Seems to know better than the hound,
The limit of its bounds; I ask,
Why else would it chance to come
Where a hound would delight
To hunt it as long as it could?

Not in fear as in annoyance
At the noisy clamor
And a canine's disrespect
Toward his master's friend
Do deer suddenly depart and disappear
In graceful leaps
And flagging goodbyes.

No talk with Noey, the hound
Named after a dear hermit
Who loved Adirondack quiet,
Will change any of that.
The harsh, barking refrain
The deer have heard before
And know there will be more;
Even so, my deer, my deer,
Are prepared for that
And will be back.

LAKE GEORGE:

ANOTHER NAME?

Why still this name, George
For our most beautiful,
Most grand Adirondack lake:
Largest within our park,
Longest too, a 32 mile stretch,
A count of 28,000 acres.

A giant lake,
A home of restless winds.

A narrow sanctuary
A hundred plus islands
Huddle in idyllic idleness.

A glance north,
A whale-mouth agape,
A long, deep, throated view;
A gorge from mountain knees gouged,
A tattered tongue midway
Reaches for sandy lips.

Adirondacker...
Who was King George,
Who to you and who to me.
Who to we now of this land
That he should be
Remembered still?

Iroquois, French and English
Mated names of choice;

What name now
For this lake supreme
Where we live and play
And die?

Time now,
A name with grace of place,
Sylvan shores, bosom hills,
Crystalline waters,
A name until creation's doom.

No more loyalty to a throne
If only in the name of a lake.
An historical reminder
Of what happened here.

Goodbye King George.
Easy in word to dismiss the dead.
A mind-set glued in time
To smooth the wrinkles of war.

No more a monarch's name
Whose royal armies fought to suppress
Birthing democracy.

No more we honor a king,
A political pet,
With a name bestowed
Though lake and king
Never met.

What say, you?

BIG TREES

Adirondack...
Grow your trees.
Grow them tall,
Grow them of wide girth,
Grow them, root them tight,
Gowth them, hold them straight.

Grow them so
Those of distant birth,
Know them.

Show them...
What sweet beauty
Time-honored trees
Bestow upon
A patient land.

THE HORSE-BARN CAMP

This old, crumbling camp
On the ragged edge
Of a grassy clearing stands:
A rectangular structure, flat and long,
Its unpeeled logs long advanced
On a path of nourishment return
For another generation of trees.

First, a rustic barn,
Then, a crude camp
Where in autumn's leafless woods
Veteran hunters gather
Around a hot drum stove
As nocturnal temperatures plunge.

Sleepers on near-ceiling bunks
Doze, warm and content,
While sleepers lower,
Too far from the big, drum stove,
Toss and turn through the night
As ground-hugging frosts
Slink from bunk to bunk.

Back-country horse barns
Once a landfall for hunters
Looking for quick, cheap camps
To house them through fall hunts,
A place to cook, eat and sleep
Feel safe from cold and rain,
Laugh where a hunter's laugh
Is best heard and understood.

Logging horses, big and strong,
Equestrian Paul Bunyons at work.

In weather, wet and cold,
Without humble shelter
Soon sick and weak,
Maybe---soon dead.

Old loggers cared,
Treated each giant horse,
As a delicate debutante in the wilds.
Rustic barns built, tight and sturdy,
Tarpaper wrapped, an extra precaution
To keep animals on the job.

A barn converted camp,
A fragrance of old hay,
The scent of horses that ate it.
Pleasant, aromatic reminders:
That once after long days
Of skidding cable-choked logs,
Or hauling sleds stacked high,
Tired woods horses rested here.

Winding, belching machines
Is what we now hear
In these North Woods.
No need for work horses;
No need for tarpaper barns.
What few still remain,
One by one, disappear.
If not by rot from bottom up,
Then, by tons of snow a-top
Pressing rafters to relent.
Or, fire finds a way.

Hunters now,
Relish luxury and convenience
In camps wherever they go.
No longer content, are most
To say: "My camp, a converted barn.
Once a bedroom for logging horses
Where now, I lay my head."

LONESOME BAY, LOWER SARANAC LAKE

A CHICKADEE DEAD

In a woodpile new, a chickadee
I found this gray day.
There it lay as dead
As anything can be,
Though a day before it fed
Just a few feet in front of me.

Why is it dead? I thought.
Do little things like this
Just die like you and I?
Was it just its time,
And so here it came to hide
And sleep 'til its end?
Or was it something more?
Surely it was not the cold
For November was still young.
Everything intact,
So it hardly seemed a victim
Of a weasel attack.
But then, I could not tell
For sure, with such a little thing.

Why did it come here
In this covered wood stack
With a forest dense so near?
Never before have I found
A chickadee at rest for good
In a pile of stove wood.

Feathers black and white,
Feathers gray,
A black-capped head,
A special distinction,
No fear, for your extinction.
Put some sunflower seeds out,
In minutes chickadees appear
Like a gang of happy bandits.
Upon the generous cache they swoop,
Plunder it 'til not a seed is left.
One seed at a time
To a nearby branch taken,
Dashed with beck to break the seal.
Not a meal, less than a snack.
A-wing again to steal
What was given them.

Chickadees so much alike,
Hard to make a special friend.
I doubt they miss the missing one.

For sameness of so many,
There's something to say,
Never just two,
A sweet serenity of family identity,
If you don't speak beyond a peep,
Or a dee-dee-dee.

A MOUNTAIN FACE

Long before they slid down your slopes
Whiteface, they called you,
A geological sage of craggy rock
Looming over the valley Ausable.

When dressed in winter's icy gowns,
No lonely glacial ghost are you.
A frenzy of activity
Upon wiggly strands of your frosty
    beard;
Hordes of human fleas
Slide well-groomed braids.

Wooden, narrow sticks no more,
High-tech skis and boards
For accelerated speed
And beauty designed.
Not a recreation for the poor,
More for those who have more.

What say you, Whiteface?
Does this activity keep you young,
Or are you sad at what has been done?
A clawing disfigurement of your breast,
A peeling of your protective skin.

Costumed as though to a coronation of a
    clown
They flock for a touch of primitive fun.
On skis monster boots attached,
On boards two feet encased on one;
Both, a one-way slide
In exchange for a one-way ride.

What say you, Whiteface?
A mountain no more so somber.
Time so long you remember.
How will you remember this day
When to the slopes they came to slide,
To bask in the arctic sun,
To frolic in the snow.

Whiteface,
Would you have it any other way.
A mountain no more so somber?

Steven & Lisa Reid Frequent skiers at Whiteface Mountain.

ANOTHER ATTITUDE

To hell with the call of the wild.
My call is the call of my crying child.
I need Pampers by the baby pound.
Bring on the big shopping mall.
Wal-Mart, K-Mart---bring them all
If it means prices slashed.
I don't care how it sounds
Or how it's done.
I want Pampers by the pound
And I want them cheap.

I want the best for my pets.
Prices chopped on canine hash
And feline mush.
Can't forget my livingroom chums.
Wilderness means nothing to them.

Can't feed a family, pay bills
On what they call---quality of life.
Surrounded by mountain scenery:
A four month cloak of green,
Six months of cold or snowy hills,
Two months of whatever.

So low the pay,
Nothing to do but stay
And enjoy unemployment.

TRILLIUM TRESSPASSERS

Dear lady, it's illegal to pick
Trilliums in the Forest Preserve.
The beauty is in leaving them
Though soon gone
And few come to see.

Pick not these trilliums on lands
Owned by the state. Don't you know
A hefty fee you'll pay, dear lady.
If a bouquet you take,
A scheduled day in court,
A stay at a county jail
If a uniform of green
With a ticket book so handy
Patrols this path this day?

No need to plea your innocence.
In your hand you hold
An admission of guilt.

Dear lady from the city
Come where trilliums grow,
By millions, I'm sure,
By thousands, I see.
On this land not owned by the state.
Set snowy petalled lips striped with red
Upon your dark, glistening hair
Without fear of lawful penalty.

A beauty short-lived,
A trillium in hand or hair.
A simple flower yours
For a sunny hour.
Touch it, love it, before it wilts.
A flower, a friend, each are we,
All soon gone.

NO PARKER ARE YOU

Adirondacker...
In a park you live
By definition of a line
Unless by chance
You're beyond the legal boundary.
By what definition...a park.

You never thought much of it
Until it loomed and bloomed
With countless demands
And firm, bureaucratic commands.
Not to defend you
From a lurking enemy,
But the park...from you.

Not a parker are you.
It's Adirondack still..
Stronger now by far.

Not a parker are you.
Come to play,
Luxuriate in solitary sun
At a sumptuous resort.

A privilege to live here,
Not a rustic prison,
Not a club of foolish clowns
Who scorn the seat they sit upon.
How to say
Surrender not right
For privilege,
Or privilege for right.
Stronger without surrender.
For the sake of beauty
Must a choice be made?

Are we, you and me,
Below all we see?

NOAH JOHN RONDEAU *

Well Noey, you made it.
On thousands of shelves,
In book, drug and stationary
Stores, stands your book.
It sells for six bucks.
Hundreds of libraries and homes
Have given you a space of honor,
Next to favorite and famous authors.
Can you imagine that?
I bet you're having a laugh.
Mr. DeSormo you have to thank.
In spite of your literary prank
Of codes and symbols,
Which no one may ever decipher,*
You could have given more
If you had not chosen
To make it a useless chore.

One summer day I tramped back
To see what was left.
I was surprised to find
Part of your small shack
Still stands on the high bluff
Above Big Dam:
Roof collapsed, sides slanted,
Wood, inside and out,
Weathered grey,
As though exposed,
For a hundred years,
To rain, snow and sun
Not as old as it looks, I thought,
For I can remember back

When we sat and talked
In this little, smoke-filled shack.

"Yes, this is the one," I say,
As I examine its innards,
"There's the soot in the cracks."
Old Noey, you had a white beard,
Tinged with yellow, when we met,
But your lungs, I bet,
Were as black as the soot
In those cracks.

How long this crumbling memorial,
Without plaque or priority,
Will last no one knows
Or really cares, I suppose,
For any tomorrow it may quickly succumb,
To the axe of a camping chum
Looking for kindling.
What does it mean to him,
This junk wood in the wilderness?
He never heard of
The hermit of the Cold River bluff.

Sweet peas, sweet peas,
Colorful survivors yet
Of your wilderness garden,
Still gives glory to the spot
Where once you planned to rest.
In the end, grasses and weeds win.
Then trees.
But they haven't won yet.
What else is left as witness
Of your stay of how many thousand days
And nights, through blizzardy winters
And insect-ridden summers?

Your larder, from the wilds
Shows no evidence,

But that which from town came
In hikers packs; now, empty
Brown, unidentifiable cans
Over the bluff lay.
Their varied contents
Many a meal fed you.
Long after the weathered shack
And blue and red sweet peas are gone
They'll remain.

Then when hikers ask,
Where's Rondeau's hermitage?
Those who know may have to say,
On the bluff above
The old corroded trash.

* Written about 1970
* Code deciphered: David Greene in 1992

One of Rondeau's huts as first displayed at the Adirondack Museum. Now found at the indoor hermitage.

A SOLDIER'S ADIRONDACK DREAM

Bunkered amid scrubby Korean hills,
I think of aromatic woods
I use to roam far from city pavements.
These long thoughts of familiar forests
Rush like mountain brooks turning pages
Of woodland scenes in my mind.

Down steep slopes,
Go gurgling rills,
So gleeful, so enslaved
In their mission to find
The nearest brook.
And when enough of solitude
And hiding they've had,
A stream they claim
Until, at last, a river,
With a destination and a dream,
They marry, and sleep
Within its womb, to await
Another awakening.

In mind and heart,
I look, I listen, smell and taste
Forest scenes as they ride on my tongue,
I absorb the beauty of a morning lake,
Waiting, serenely and patiently,
For us to communicate again.
Each moment, a new scene...
Morning sun with golden promise,
Noon brightness dispelling all
Hint of darkness here or beyond,
Evening sun fading from sight
Like a slow sad abandonment
Of earth and all upon it.

Beauty in nature, a capricious cloud,
So temporary, so quickly replaced
Like troops on the battle line,
That, in the fire of time, fall.
Beauty sublime...
Only in the heart,
Only in the mind,
Only in a dream alive,
A dream open and free
To the reality of time.

Once more may I haunt
With canoe and paddle, boots and pack,
These mountain lakes and rivers,
These forests green and fragrant
When I get back;
See them all again:
Lovely faces and lonely places
In the wild Adirondacks.

Chorwon, Korea 1952

One of several "hoochie" homes of author while serving in Korea

Much of Korea is a bare mountainous country but lacks a great forest as found in the Adirondacks.

LOST POND, PHARAOH LAKE WILDERNESS

NEW

ACQUAINTANCE

Another pond I found
Without long search or pain;
A vacuum, as it were, of tranquility
A sprint in spirit and step
From vehicles accelerating,
Expelling whiffs of fumy smoke
In haste to ascend Graphite Mountain.
Wheels squealing on smooth pavement
Unearthly sounds shatter silence
Of nearby woods.

Serenity in snacks of time
Sandwiched between noisy bursts.
A walk in waning light
In wilds never before seen
Now still remembered.

Words spoken with none to listen.
Searching for a treasure unsure,
A moment to pleasantly recall.

From this secluded place,
Just before a fair exchange
From sun to moon, I took
A glimpse of water still
Looking to the night
Without a human shelter in sight.

Only creatures wild now live here,
A ragged dome of pointed sticks
A near shore residence.
On bark and leaf they subsist
Throughout the year. No need
For more than they have here.

Once this land a rage to satisfy
An industry now defunct.
Walk its maze,
Steal from pockets of tranquility
Morsels of serenity. Quick snacks
For future consumption
When spirits crave
Serenity of scene and soul.

A FAMILIAR REFRAIN

Adirondacker...
You've heard it
When you weren't meant to hear it;
You've heard it
From people you wish had not said it;
You've heard it
Where it was daring to say it.

When Adirondack reformers gather
To discuss what should
Or should not be done,
In chorus soon they agree
And sing this familiar refrain
Of righteous encouragement:

Oooooh, let's save the Adirondacks
from the nasty Adirondackers.
Destroy it they will, if we let them.
Only if we let them, we let them.
Of course we know what is best for them
Is not best for our Adirondacks.
Oh my, oh my, we'll tell you why
We'll tell you, tell you why,
If you send us some money,
And in your will, remember us.
Trust us, to save the Adirondacks
From those who live there.

Look, a peace-rupturing raptor
With whirling wings,
On a lustful mission.
Apprehend nature's outlaws
Who, in a stoop-to-enter shanty, sleep
Where screech owls and coyote packs
Howl in the night.

No asphalt spread to smooth the path;
No trees downed to improve the view;
No millions on septic spent
For nature housed within
And upon a colorful, dancing screen
    displayed.

What threat, Adirondackers,
Thirteen to a square mile
Before the summer crowd here arrives?

AN EVENING CALL

Wood thrush...
I cannot speak
Your language sweet;
So tenderly delivered
In fading, evening light.

Your cheer...
A song short and clear;
A song so dear
I cannot sing or say
How much it means to me.

Others too of wing...
Send notes high and long,
Now silent, now listen.

A closing gift,
Your musical reverie,
To a day you found right;
A promise sure
To happily greet another
With emerging, morning light.

HERE TO STAY

Here by birth,
Here by choice,
Here by mere circumstance,
Here, because here is where you are.

What difference does it make why
If here is where you want to be,
And here you plan to stay,
And here you call yourself
An Adirondacker...

Not for play, not for place,
Not for pride, not for people,
For these all;
A call to belong
To a wild land
Where a heart song
Calls in its sounds
And in its silences.

An Adirondacker...
Here by birth,
Here by choice,
Here, because here is where you are
And here you plan to stay.